ROYAL POLISH LETTERS

1350-1360 AD

Casimir IV
King of Rus' and Poland
Translated by: D.P. Curtin

Copyright @ 2022 Dalcassian Press

All rights reserved. No part of this publication may be reproduced, distributed, or transmitted in any form or by any means, including photocopying, recording, or other electronic or mechanical methods, without the prior written permission of the publisher, except in the case of brief quotations embodied in critical reviews and certain other non-commercial uses permitted by copyright law. For permission request, write to Dalcassian Press at dalcassianpublishing at gmail.com

ISBN: 979-8-3302-0354-3 (Paperback)

Library of Congress Control Number:
Author: Curtin, D.P. (1985-)

Printed by Ingram Content Group, 1 Ingram Blvd, La Vergne, Tennessee

First printing edition 2022.

ROYAL POLISH LETTERS

Kalis, March, 29, 1350

The king confirms a certain special article of privilege, from his father Vladislaus, Governor of the hospital of the Holy Spirit given in Kalisz, in which the right of fishing of the aforesaid hospital had been expressed.

We, Casimir, king of Poland by the grace of God, publicly declare both the present and the future, that the honorable man and brother Kerstanus, master of the hospital of the Holy Spirit in Kalis, approached our presence and requested us most urgently, that the privilege of the same hospital over different liberties and rights through our progenitor, Lord Wladyslaw of happy memory, who was once made ruler of the kingdom of Greater Poland, we would deign to confirm, in which privilege one article among the others, which was as follows: we allow the same fisherman to be kept in the hospital: it was contained. This article, for the honor and praise of Almighty God and the Holy Spirit, and for the salvation of our souls and the remission of sins, is more favorably inclined to the just and worthy prayers of the aforesaid brother Kerstan, that no impediment to the aforesaid hospital be imposed by anyone in the article of fishing permanently granted and granted to the same hospital , by special grace and usual piety, we confirm that this series of letters will prevail for ever and ever. But if anyone, by a reckless venture, presumes to disturb or hinder the said hospital in the fisherman or article of fishing, let him feel that he has incurred our indignation grievously. Done at Kalis on the second day below the eighth of Pascha, in the year of the Lord one thousand three hundred and fifty, in the presence of these witnesses: Iarando Castellan of Rospiri, captain of Siradien, Otto of Polonie, Florian of Lancicia, chancellors, and many other trustworthy persons. Given by the hands of our aforesaid chancellor, Sir Otto, and written by the notary of our court, Pribislaus, and the prefect of the church of the blessed George at Gneznam.

Poznan, April 13, 1350

He grants to the inhabitants of the towns of the church of Poznan all freedom from all the exactions of his dominion, as long as the bishop himself has bestowed it upon them.

Let it be made manifest to all and everyone to whose notice the present writing has been presented, that we, Casimir, by the grace of God, king of Poland, from the duty granted to us by God, desire to extend the interests of our kingdom more widely, so that from this the present and our future progress may grow richer and more fervent. and that what the density of the forests of the war has uncovered with the help of the war, may be reformed by the grace and power of freedom: therefore, having a special zeal and devotion to the church of blessed Peter in Poznań, and by the petitions of the venerable father of Lord Albert in Christ, by the grace of God, the bishop of the same church of Poznań, more favorably disposed to the just and worthy, to all and to each kmeton and inhabitants in the districts underwritten and the villages all situated in them, namely Pczew, Wylcyna, Buk with the adjacent village, Welychova, Zambrszko, Croba, Bane, with all their territories and adjacent areas, but specially and expressly located in the villages of Wythassyce and Slessyno heretofore and in future leases, from all our payments, exactions, contributions, grievances, arrears, pre-angares, labors, conveyances whatsoever and collected in general to all by whatever name they may be called, as long as the same lord bishop, abstaining from his assessments and payments, has given a similar liberty, and for so long We are also graciously given to them. Indeed, if anyone presumes to infringe upon this liberty by a rash venture, he knows that he has incurred our indignation grievously. Given in Poznań on the third week after the Sunday on which the Lord's Mercy is sung, in the year of the same.

May 19, 1350

About the monastery of Suleyow; Peczconi, a citizen of Wrocław, sells the advowson of the city of Łęczyca together with the rights of the same, and establishes him as a hereditary advowson there.

In the name of the Lord, amen. It is worthy and honorable that what the authority of princes has decreed to be done, should be observed permanently and irrevocably. Therefore let both the present age and the future know that Casimir, king of Poland by the grace of God, as well as the lord and heir of the lands of Krakow, Sandomierz, Syradia, Lancic, Cuyavia, and Pomerania, because of the needs generally occurring to us and to our kingdom, will summon us in our city of Lancic with all right and with regard to the possession of the same, we sold and resigned to a prudent and honorable man Peczcon, a citizen of Wratislavia, for one hundred and fifty marks of gross Prague, to hold, hold, give, sell, exchange and possess for himself and his true heirs and legitimate successors forever and irrevocably, for his and to be converted by the will of his posterity: these rents were expressly given to him by the same plea, that is to say, three free manors in the city itself and three similarly free in the town of Thopola, adding four free butcher's butchers: which, indeed, the town of Thopola should be enjoyed and rejoiced by the same right as the city of Lancic is situated. We also give to the aforesaid advocate and to his posterity a third part of all the camels, of the linen cloths, or of the pressed cloths, of the bread or cakes, of the tailors, and of the fish; past the shops and fields of the city and the annual market, in which the aforesaid advocate shall retain no interest. We also allow the same attorney to make all the benefits for his own benefit that he can devise by allowing the law of the New Market, of which he will have a third penny, two reserved for us. We wish to say that no judge of the Palatines, Castilians, or any of the citizens of our kingdom should judge for any cause or causes great or small, such as theft, bloodshed, murder, arson, and all other things, except the aforesaid lawyer and his successors. The aforesaid advocate and his heirs shall in no way answer before the aforesaid palatine, castellan, and judge, who were for the time being; but only before us, as long as they have been summoned by a letter protected by our seal, then they will answer those who complain about themselves by the Teutonic law. Also, we will and decree that the aforesaid attorney and his successors shall be obliged to serve in every expedition for the defense of our kingdom with one man in plates and slappa. Moreover, the provincial, who is called lanthwoyth, or our procurator, will preside over great trials three times a year, according to custom and custom. In the testimony and clearest evidence of all of them, we have given the present, strengthened by the protection of our seal. Done in the stations around the monastery of Suleyow in our conference on Wednesday below the eighth of Pentecost, in the year of the Lord one thousand three hundred and fifty, in the presence of these witnesses: Spicimir castellan of Krakow, Nicholas palatine of Kalisiens, Iarando castellan of Rosperian and captain of Syradiens, Michael the butler, Philip the sub-chamberlain, Stephen Rola the assistant of Lancic , and many others. Given by the hand of Lord Florian, chancellor of Lancic.

ROYAL POLISH LETTERS

Krakow, June 21, 1352

To the church of Gneznes, for the sum of two thousand marks, which he had received from his own treasury in various ornaments, he assigned one hundred marks to the annual census of the Prague merchants to be collected from the soups in Bochnia and Wieliczka.

In the name of the Lord, amen. Since the deeds of princes, rationally ordered, are bound to remain firm and intact for all time, and therefore must be commended to the notice of the letters of the tips with the annotation of the witnesses of posterity, therefore we Casimir, by the grace of God, king of Poland and also of the lands of Krakow, Sandomierz, Syradie, Lancicia, Cuyavia, Pomorania, and lord of Russia and heirs, we make it known to all present and future, to whose notice the present writing has reached, that in the greatest necessity falling upon us and our kingdom, we have received from the treasury of the church of Gnezna, in the deliberation of our barons, crosses, tables, cups, and other ornaments of gold and pearls for two thousand marks of the weight of Polish silver, which, crushed and fused, we decided to convert for the benefit of our kingdom. But because the same money has not yet been paid by us to the church of Gneznes itself, even in some part paid, we turn our consciences in the closet of our hearts with urgent meditation, how we can return the same church of Gneznes in its treasury indemnified and save our conscience. Now, therefore, having called to our presence for this purpose our venerable father Lord Bozatha, Bishop of Krakow, and his Chapter, and the noblemen John of Sandomiri and Ymram Palatine of Krakow, and Wylczcon, castellan of Sandomiri, also consuls of our city of Krakow, we had with them the service of counsel concerning the premises; by the use of whose advice and deliberation with us, to a careful, healthy mind and body, we gave, we give, and even assign to the present perpetually, in repayment of the debt pre-assessed, to the said church of Gneznes and to our venerable father Lord Jaroslaw, now the archbishop of Gneznes, not by error, but by spontaneous and free will , and to his successors, the archbishops of Gneznes, to receive one hundred marks of Prague gross, counting forty-eight gross for each mark, from our soup in Bochna and Weliczka in ready money every year, by themselves or through their representatives whom they have brought here to be deputed: fifty marks at the festival blessed Stanislaus after Easter, and another fifty marks on the feast of blessed Michael the Archangel: notwithstanding any contradiction or occasion. Mandating in the name of us and our successors from now on to our cupbearer or cupbearers, whether they were purchasers or commissioners, of whatever condition they may be, to govern the said soups at the succeeding time: inasmuch as the same money of one hundred marks, without requisition from us to any of the said church and lord archbishop of Gneznen, or to his successors who for the time being, to his or his agents specially assigned or deputed for this purpose, for perpetual periods as is a perpetual donation, they must give, present, and assign in full every year within the terms pre-assessed, so that the debt contracted by us may be compensated, and the lord archbishop with the clergy they are further obliged to pray for the remedy of our souls and of our ancestors. Moreover, if the shopkeeper or the shopkeepers, the purchasers or the commissioners, do not pay the pre-taxed money of one hundred marks in the above terms through their own rashness, we submit them of our own free will to pay the same money by ecclesiastical censure by the authority of the lord archbishop of Gnezn, who for the time being or were to be paid, notwithstanding if the same cupbearers existed in the diocese of Krakow, when the aforesaid bishop gave us free power to excommunicate, suspend, and otherwise impose ecclesiastical censure at our request, as the archbishop shall see fit, with the consent of his Chapter.

But we, the aforesaid bishop Bozatha, with the consent of our brothers of the chapter of the church of Krakow, have given to our venerable brother, Lord Jaroslaw, the archbishop of Gneznes, and to his successors, and we give all our authority to excommunicate, suspend, and otherwise compel by ecclesiastical censure the said suppers, whether they have been embezzlers or commissioners of any condition, to pay a pre-taxed sum of one hundred marks at the appointed terms.

Moreover, in order that our aforesaid donation may be commended in the church of Gneznes by prayers and vigils for the salvation of us and our ancestors and not only our successors, we have expressly agreed, agreed and preordained with the same lord archbishop and chapter of the church of Gneznes aforesaid: that on the Sabbath days mass of to the Blessed Virgin, and on Wednesdays at the vigil of the Nine Lessons, and on Fridays, Mass for the Departed, with prayer at any hour for the salvation of us and our successors, specially imposed upon the said lord archbishop and his Chapter, voluntarily and gratuitously accepting, shall be celebrated aloud every week at perpetual times. In order that this ordinance and satisfaction of ours may obtain the strength of a perpetual firmness, we have ordered the present to be written and communicated under the affixing of the seals of our superior and faithful ones above written. Done at Krakow on the Thursday after the day of the blessed martyrs of Vith and Modesti, in the year of the Lord one thousand three hundred and fifty-second, in the presence of these witnesses: Sbygneus of Krakow, Othone of Poland the chancellor, John of Woynice, Setegius of Rosperian of the castellans, Peter the tribune, Andrew the sub-chamberlain of Krakow, and Zavissius the heir of Cowale. and many others worthy of trust. Given by the hands of Sbygne, our chancellor aforesaid.

Costan, Feb. 12, 1353

Confirms the privilege he had given to the monastery of Lubin

In the name of the Lord, amen. The authority which the kings have decreed to be magnificent must continue forever in a fair and stable manner. Accordingly, we Casimir, by the grace of God, king of Poland, as well as lord and heir of the lands of Krakow, Sandomierz, Syradia, Lancicia, Cuyavia, and Pomerania, wish to make known to all present and future inspectors the present letter, that in the presence of us and our barons, the religious man brother Andrew, abbot of the holy monastery Marie in Lubyn of the Order of St. Benedict, offered us a certain privilege of our attawi, of the happy memory of Boleslay, the illustrious Duke of Poland, on the forum of the city of Crivin, humbly asking that it be confirmed by our grace.

We, therefore, having been favorably disposed to the petitions of the aforesaid abbot of the monastery, as being worthy to be more kindly inclined, having in all respects the aforesaid privilege with all its clauses and approving it as acceptable, we ratify from certain knowledge and confirm that it will last for ever and ever. desiring and deciding, by the consent and will of the abbot aforesaid, that the fair of the above-mentioned festival of Pentecost should be celebrated in our city; let our captain or palatine, or the castellan of Crivinus, or any other person, intrude upon our citizens by any civil right, or usurp any authority or power; but by payment of the market, he should give up his power entirely to the abbot and the monastery. But if anyone violates these decrees of ours, harassing people coming to Crivin with the grace of selling and removing (sic), taking away their belongings for the sake of public plunder, and obstructing the daily market through violence and violation of our decree, it is said that we and our posterity will suffer the penalty of sedmdesant. and he shall pay to the abbot the penalty, which is called pencznazescze, which shall last for ever and ever.

He summoned the act in Costan on the third day after Sunday, in the year of the Lord 1350, in the presence of noble men: Maczkone pallatino of Poznań,

Andrea of Kalisiensi, Vincencio of Strzemensi, Benyamyn of Gneznensi, Czestkone of Costrina, Woyslao of Drozine, Iasco of Crivina of Castilian, and several others worthy of trust. Given by the hands of Mr. Florian, our chancellor of Lancic.

Poznan, February 16, 1353

The parish of Owińska contributes the villages of Skorzęcin and Barcinek.

In the name of the Lord, amen. It is worthy that those things which the royal majesty has decided to do with good motion for the benefit of the welfare of the present as well as of the future, should always obtain the strength of firmness. Therefore we Casimir, by the grace of God, king of Poland, as well as of Krakow, Sandomierz, Siradi, Lanzic, Cuyavia, and Pomeranian lands, lord and heir, with the present and future notice of all the worlds declare by this writing that considering the extreme scarcity and need of religious and dedicated virgin sisters of the convent of the Owensko Order To the Cistercians, situated and situated in the territory of Poznań, for the reparation of the souls of our parents and for our own special salvation, we give, confer and donate to the aforesaid monastery two villages, namely, Curzancino and Barchcino, with all their fruits, rents, revenues, waters, meadows, pastures and all other interests, with every right and interest as we alone held, to hold and hold and possess in perpetuity and inheritance. And lest by any man our gift should be violated in posterity, we made presents to be given, strengthened by the protection of our seal. The act of Poznan on the Sabbath before the Sunday on which the song is sung Reminiscere, in the year of the Lord one thousand three hundred and fifty-three, in the presence of these witnesses: Iaroslaus, archbishop of Gneznen, Albert, bishop of Poznan, Nicholas Palatine of Kalisien, Pretslaus the castellan of Poznan, and Sandivogio of Nakl and Vincentius of the castellan of Srzemensi, and many other trustworthy persons.

Given by the hands of Florian, our chancellor of Lancic.

Prague, May 1, 1356

Treaty with Charles, king of the Romans. He also renews and enlarges the entry of Namslavia, by the vigor of which the king had said, if he could recover the boundaries of the kingdom of Poland against the Order of the House of the Teutonic Order and the Marquis of Brandenburg, with the vigor of which he promised to render aid against anyone, except King Louis of Hungary.

Casimir, by the grace of God, king of Poland and Russia, as well as the lord and heir of the lands and duchies of Krakow, Sandomierz, Sirade, Lancicia, Cuiavia, and Pomerania, we make it known to all: that because the most serene and invincible prince and lord Charles, ever august emperor of the Romans and king of Bohemia , to our dearest brother, in the treaties held between his majesty, on the one side, and us on the other, in his town of Nampslavia, under the year of the Lord 2348, the first indictment, on the tenth of the Calends of December, in the third year of his reign, under the title of Roman king which he used at that time , we duly promised under an oath: thus and now, with the deliberate and mature mind of our forefathers' previous counsel, we promise under the same oath to observe perpetual love and firm friendship inviolably to all in the times to come, just as he conversely returned to us under the oath previously lent to the observance of the same love and Let him be bound by friendship, as is more fully contained in the ancient letters of our concord between us and him. The aforesaid Lord Emperor also promised, under an oath taken before him, in good faith and without guile, against any man, and specifically against the Crusaders of the Teutonic house, or even against the Bavarians or any others remaining in the Marquisate of Brandenburg, or in his own person, if it could conveniently be done. or in the person of the illustrious prince Lord John Marquis of Moravia, his brother, to assist with six hundred men in helmets and to be suffocated amicably; at that particular time, when the plants and crops are in the fields. And if any of the enemies should invade our lands at any time before the time of the harvest, he promised, under the premise of an oath, without guile, that he would be able to help us against the attack of those enemies of ours with all his might. And if the first time with the same men we did not recover the limits of our kingdom against our enemies, then secondarily he promised to assign us four hundred helmets at our request, and he would be held under his damages, costs and expenses; so, however, that we are bound and promised to provide his aforesaid army with food and drink, as long as he tarries in our kingdom. And if, as we do not expect, we should not recover the boundaries of the same kingdom the first and second time, then the third and fourth time, and whenever necessary, he has promised us under oath and faith to vote according to his ability without deception, and he is bound to do so as long as we recover the boundaries of our kingdom as aforesaid . Having recovered them, we shall be obliged to assist and defend the aforesaid lord the emperor and the kingdom of Bohemia against every man, except the king of Hungary, as is expressed in our ancient letters. Moreover, as long as we had not achieved success against our enemies, we were not obliged to support them. I add this, however, that, in the meantime and in the meantime, we will not cooperate with his enemies through us or ours to assist them with the same help, advice, or favor, and the aforesaid helmets, which he is obliged to assign to our assistance, must be at his own expense and expense, and the reimbursement of damages without deceit. to look back until the said limits have returned to our domain. Thus, the boundaries of the kingdom of Poland having been obtained in some way by their vote, the occupiers of the goods and dominions not belonging to our kingdom of Poland have been conquered and expelled, half of those goods and dominions to the aforesaid lord the emperor and the king of Bohemia, but the remainder we decide to apply to our own uses. And everything and every detail that is known to be contained in these letters of ours, word for word, as expressed there, we promise to observe inviolably to each letter and we are bound under all the ways and conditions, as expressed in the same letters, under the dates, place and time specified. with the sole exception that of all the moneys of which they constitute a mention in the same letter, the said Lord Emperor, the King of Bohemia, and his sureties and compromisers are completely and completely absolved, as the Most Serene Prince Louis King of Hungary, our dearest brother, the aforesaid Lord Emperor and the King of Bohemia, and we, his sureties and conciliators, according to the likeness of the said King of Hungary, by our special letters, have duly quitted and released the children, and completely absolved them. But if, being absent, he fails to make or send us the aforesaid vote as required by us, then for the same vote, as often as he neglects to do so, he or his sons, if any he had by the Lord's permission, or by him having died without heirs, the illustrious prince John Marquis of Moravia, his brother aforesaid, in the event that he succeeds to himself in the kingdom of Bohemia, we shall and will be able to admonish him. Presented under the seal of our majesty as evidence of letters.

Done and given at Prague in the year of the Lord 1356, on the day of the blessed apostles Philip and James.

Krakow, March 1, 1357

He confirms all the rights, privileges, liberties and donations granted to the church of Gneznes by anyone.

In the name of the Lord, amen. It is known that it would be worthy and consistent with reason that the alma mater holy church of Gnezna, just as in the kingdom of Poland by metropolitan law presides over all the churches, so the prerogative of honor should be decorated with a greater privilege by the grace of a singular one. Accordingly, we Casimir, by the grace of God, king of Poland, and also the lord and heir of Krakow, Sandomierz, Syradi, Lancicia, Cuiavia, and Pomorania, we wish to bring to the notice of all present and future worlds, that our venerable father in Christ, Lord Jaroslaus, by the same grace, the archbishop of the holy church of Gnezna, coming with their Chapter to our presence, they humbly and devoutly explained to us, that because the privileges of the same church, granted to them by the illustrious masters, the kings and princes of Poland, in which rights and liberties were fully contained, some of them had been consumed by their antiquity, but some by the wars If they had been destroyed by disturbances and cremations, we would design to provide them and the church with the aforesaid royal majesty for an opportune remedy; that we may mercifully command that privileges which have been spent be renewed, those which have been lost be restored, and others reformed. We, however, nodding favorably to their just and reasonable supplications, in the manner of a pious patron, when there is a law examined by kings and princes, the churches and ecclesiastical persons, especially in whom they have the right of patronage, to paternal counsel, protect and endow, held with us in deliberation and with our barons, on a sufficient premise treaty, to the honor of Almighty God and the blessed Virgin Mary and to the glory of Saint Adalbert the martyr and glorious pontiff patron of the church of Gnezna, and with a view to eternal retribution, considering also the merits of honesty and numerous services constantly presented and invested to us by the aforesaid lord archbishop: each and every privilege, liberties, concessions and donations, of whatever tenor and form they exist, by whomever or by whomever they have been given, granted and donated to the church of Gneznes, we confirm in the name of the Lord from certain knowledge, and we strengthen them with the present privilege with perpetual validity. Moreover, desiring to follow in the footsteps of our forefathers, who endowed the same church of Gnezne with many graces, and to make greater grace for the same church, so that it may be enlarged in rights under the crown of our government, and that the lord archbishop himself with his clergy, pour out prayers for our safety and for the souls of our forefathers all the goods of Gneznensis itself and of the other collegiate churches, that is, of Lancic, Rudensis, Kurzelovian, and Uneovian, and of the parochial churches of the diocese of Gneznensis, whether they be towns or inheritances, whether villages or camps, which we have now for greater certainty in the present privilege described by their proper names : First, namely, all the areas around the church of Gneznes, which the prelates, canons and vicars now own, with the rise and the two houses around the blessed Peter. Also, Kandzerzyno, Virzbiczani, Szczitniky with lots adjacent to the same, Manczerzino, Slavno with lots adjacent to it, Ostrovsko, Czatome, Lubcza, Queczyssow city with market, Goressovo, Sedlimovice. And in the district of Znen, the city of Znen with its forum, Sarbinovo, Byscupino with adjacent lots, Czaple, Ianczevo, Gorice, Golcevo, Dochunevo, Sulimovo, Rybitvi, Prescoristew, Dobrilevo, Chomantovo, Sandovo, Vilczcovo, Vrzuty, Murzino, Gora, Balovezino, Pnevo , Luthcovo before Pacoscz, Pothgorzino, Rylevo and Scarbinice. In the territory of Nakel: Wavriscovo, Plocyce, Czirekvicza and the village church of Nakel called Konotoppa. Also, in the land of Kalissia: Opatow, Zduni, Troyanovo, two Godzessovo, Glovczino, Woycovo, Solecz, Transovo, Warsovo, Lisconice, Zytovice, Kokanino and Ilme. Also, on the other side of the river Przosna: Noscovo, Byskupice around Olobok, Byskupice called Smolky, Bukovnicza, Svanthcoviczy, Gyzice and Byskupice called Kothlovo, and Sovina. Also, in the land of Velunsi: Sencza, Raduienice, Lyssovicy, two lots in our village Bobrovniky, Kamona, Kadlub, Gana, Broza, Zalancz and Vydrzyno. In the castellan of Landes: Czarncovo, Grzegorovo city with forum, Kelczovo, Scovelice, Bogussina Woda, Rzuchovo; Czissove, Grambcovo from the other side of the river Warte. Also, in the land of Cuiavie: two Uyma, Byskupice near Radzeow, Smogorzow, and two lakes called Chotle and Bezdzedze between the town of Chotle and Comoro. Kulin in the land of Dobrinense. Also these villages in the land of Lancic: the village around the church with the allodium, called Chothnicza, Thomino with the site of the mill, Podgorzyce, Mchovice, Moracovo, the city of Pantek with the market, Lubnicza, Mancolici, Zduny; Bancovo, Gyzice, Slonevo, which three towns are united into one town called Bancovo; Viskithnicza, Lanzsniky, Symunovice, Marzicze, Struginice, Verzenovice, Gavroni with the adjacent village called

Sulcovo, Sanczcovo, Lanka, Czecerzino, Peczevo, Chelm, Sobothka with a bridge commonly called mostove, Crzikossy, Slupcza, Koczave, Rudultovo, Solcza minor, Gutovo, in Topola military two lots, Crzepoczino, Parundzice, and in Zdun four lots, Prussinovice, Svarava. Three lots in great Leznicia. In Wozniky there are four lots and a shop. In Gambice two lots, Mrozovice, Solecz with an adjacent town called Pracze. Between Blone and Dambe there is one lot called Dulovo. Three lots in Wyssoke, one lot between Milovice and Lyczky. Also, in Jancovo, Miroslavice, Sdzechovo, in the half of Czirzchow, Sosnka, Chranstow, Dobrogostovice, Grambinice and Grabissevo. Also, these towns in the land of Syradia: the city of Uneyow with the market and the town connected to it called Koscelnaves, Ostrovsko, Wola Czichmana, Sbilucycze, Orzeskovo, Velenino, Kobilniky, Ubislave, Nemislow with the town of Lubiscovo, Popovo, Karchovo, Zarovo, Borissovice. In Marzanino part of the chancellery of Gneznensis, Sandzeyovice, Luceyow, Parzno, Strezovo, Creslovo, Drozdzino, Potrukozy, Kluky, Ressotarzevo, Rzansna, Macoviscza, Okradzissevo, Rzuievicy with Wola called Crzomech, Golcovice, Grocholice. Also on the other side of the river Warte: Spycimirz, Velscycze, Smolsco, Przykuna, Koritcovo, Rogow, Kovale, Turcovicy, the city of Turek with the market and two villages attached to it, Sencze with some fields from Muchnino, Dobrovo, Goszczonovicze, part of Tandovo, Dusniky, Kokosky, Oraczovo, Iarocyce and Oveczky. Also, these towns in the land of Krakow: Byskupicy near Mechovia with the town called Lgota adjacent to it, Prussy before Krakow, Chrosczina near Koscelecz. Also, these towns in the land of Sandomierz: the city of Kurzelow with the market and the tenth weekly tax and with the allodium called Modrzew, Gosczancin with the middle tax of the bridge and with the iron factory called Szup, Wzlecza, Dankow, Koneczno, Cyrno, Crolevice before Vislicia. Also these towns of the Chapter of Gneznensis: Decanovice, two Pisczino, Szczavino, Braczessevo, decanate fields outside Gneznam, Mnichovo, Pavlovo, Kampel, Zydovo, Valissevo, Parczevo, Popcovo, Byskupice, Iezercza, Marzanino, Gozdovo, Ksanzno, Baranovo, Opatovo, Cyrnelino two, more and less, Sulovo, Wlostovo, Smecyscza, in Manczniky three lots, Lubrza, Gosczissino, Budzislave, Slavomirz, Voyucino, Scepancovo, two Parlino, Berlino, Polanovo, Ostrovite, Zlothcovo, Scarbimirzice, Kayovo, Marquarce, Tropessino, Woycyce, Ostrow, Slup, Skvolno, Pampovo, Pampycy or Kopydlovo, Czosram. Also, the Village of sanctuaries, Komorovo Jezerzani, Crzinka, Kocycze, Mokrzsco, Dusno and Galanzovo. Also, Malonovo near Turek. In Rozdzice land in Lancic four lots and a tavern, in Domanovo one lot. Of course, we release the very good premises and completely free and gracefully absolve them from our and the camp's summons, and from our judgment and that of all the palatines, captains, castellans, judges, sub-judicials, and any officials, by whatever names they may be called; It is commonly said, that the goods themselves and those who inhabit them should be specially free and exempt; but the lord archbishop and his Chapter of Gnezna, who were for the time being, will place their justiciary in the goods of the church, who will diligently visit the same goods of the church, and restrain those who inhabit them from excesses, and correct them by means of justice. But if, beyond the knowledge of the same, our justice perceives any thief in the aforesaid goods of the church, he must refer him to the aforesaid justice of the church, who shall render justice in respect of the same. Indeed, the justiciar of the church has the power to receive punishments on men of the church, theft, bloodshed and murder, on those who have been judicially condemned; to which our justiciar has absolutely no respect, as is preferred. Furthermore, we grant and confirm to the aforesaid lord archbishop and his successors every opportunity to dispose of the said goods and possessions of the church according to the Teutonic law, as they shall see fit. And these goods and possessions, as they are contained in their circumferences, with all the benefits, fruits, and proceeds of all things, both present and future, with fields, meadows, woods, meadows, redwoods, worts, beekeeping, forests, and with the hunting of all kinds of beasts and birds. mills, ponds, lakes, and water-courses, and generally with all the uses which are now or may be in the future in the same goods, with the people inhabiting the same, both free and subject, we release, free, and discharge graciously from all payments, exactions, collections , such contributions and taxes, not only from podvorove, from poradlne, from a fence, from an ox, from a cow, from a pig, from a sheep, from a ham, from a stan, from a narzaz, from a przevod, from a povod, and from all angaris and from extortions and harassments of any kind, from all service and servitude, and especially from the digging of ditches, and from the building of camps newly made or being made, beyond the ancient camps, that is to say, in Gnezna, in Lancicia, in Syradz, and in Nakel, which while it happened to fall , the men of the church were bound to reform each of their camps from two huts; nor should they be completely exempt from expeditions emerging outside the borders of the kingdom of Poland. We wish, however, that if at any time our enemies invade the lands (sic) of our diocese of Gnezne in a hostile manner, the men of the church nearer to the part of the land which should have been invaded, together with our natives and their villeins, ready as the villeins of the soldiers themselves, should be obliged to meet the same enemies. Moreover, we add by decreeing that the soldiers should not hinder or prevent the rent in the granges of their peasants and the free sale of tithes, lest on this account God be provoked: since, according to natural law, he ought to be free to dispose of his own property as he pleases. We decide, however, that when the tithes should have been sold by their owners to strangers, it is permissible for the heirs to reserve the tithes themselves in their own villages, for the same amount of money for which they have been exposed to others, for their own use. so, however, that if the foreign buyer chooses to give the master a tenth of the money prepared at the beginning of his purchase, he is also bound to pay the same money prepared to him without delay as the heir of the town. But if such a foreign buyer has put up a surety bond for such money, the same heir of the estate must put up a surety bond of this kind on his behalf. We also declare that we find the archbishop of Gneznes and his church in the possession and receipt of the theloney for the tenth week in our underwritten towns and cities, namely in Kalis and Lancicia, in Potrcovia, in Syradz, in Malogoscz, in Chanczin, in Spyczimirz, in Skrzyn and in Chocessow, so we desire them to remain perpetually in the perception of this tenth week of the aforesaid peaceably and quietly. In the meantime, we specifically decide that if anyone in the aforesaid Gneznis and its aforesaid collegiate churches commits any notorious violence in matters or persons, the same shall be addressed by the aforesaid lord archbishop and his successors to a satisfactory ecclesiastical censure. Moreover, if a man belonging to the goods of the church, free or subject, is killed by another of our men or a soldier, the custom of paying a fine on the capital of the lands in which the murders are committed shall be observed. We wish, however, that the people of the church should be completely exempted from payment, which is called zaglovna or krvava, sescz grziven in the common language, and paid. Likewise, we decree that those who have been excommunicated shall be expelled from the court by the judge, and they shall not be admitted to testify, provided that this is not done fraudulently. We further order and desire that it be observed, that concerning the limitations of the possessions or inheritances of the churches set forth above, the custom of the church and of any land which has hitherto existed shall be observed. Likewise, we grant to the same lord archbishop and his successors that they may, even absent from court, appoint a procurator, or procurators, or spokesmen, in hereditary cases, to act and defend, to investigate or to destroy, and this by letters confirmed by their seals: when he himself is known to have hereditary possessions in different territories of our kingdom. Furthermore, what is stated last, is recommended more to memory: we decide and order and of the rest by us and everyone we want to be constantly observed: that the lord archbishop and his own of Gneznis and others named above the church with the clergy and people living in the good church, comfortable in rights and customs and touching the honor of the churches, and especially in the rights granted and given to them by us, they shall be fully preserved. We further protest that we have seen and fully understood the letters of the most blessed fathers of the Roman pontifical church, namely, Innocent the second, Innocent the third, and Honorius the third, in which the possessions, rights and liberties of the aforesaid Gnezna and its collegiate churches were granted and given to them by the princes The Poles, our progenitors, are most fully confirmed; and we have seen especially in the open letters of the said Pope Honorius to contain quite clearly, that he, at the request of the undersigned dukes, Lestcon of Krakow, Conrad of Masovia, Vladislaus of Kalis, and Casimir of Opol, confirmed the rights, liberties, and possessions of the district of Lovica, the land of Masovia, and the district itself with He completely freed all the towns and possessions from all the jurisdiction and dominion of any princes. We declare, indeed, for the purpose of cutting off the aforesaid article or clause concerning the excommunicated (sic): that if an excommunicated person is produced as a witness, he is rejected, as was promised, from testifying; but nevertheless, another witness may be substituted in his place, lest by this means any prejudice be generated to the one producing the witnesses. And in order that our aforesaid innovation, confirmation, reinforcement, protest, and perpetuation of all the premises may obtain the strength of perpetual firmness, we have caused the present letter to be written and fortified with the protection of our seals. Act of Krakow on the eighth day of the Ashes, in the year of the Lord one thousand three hundred and fifty-seven, in the presence of these witnesses, the lords John Iura the castellan of Krakow, Mathias of Poznan, Imbramo of Krakow and John of Lancic, Preczslao of Poznan, Dobeslao of Wisliciens, Zawissa of Sandecsen and John of Woyniciens and Chebda of Syradiensi castellan, Peter the tribune and Andrea the sub-chamberlain of Krakow, and Dobeslaus the judge of Kalissia; nor John of Krakow, Otto of Polonie, Florian of Lancicie, and Herman Cuiavie, chancellors of the lands of our kingdom, and many others worthy of trust. Given by the hand of the same John, chancellor of Krakow, written by the hand of Gregory, notary of our court.

ROYAL POLISH LETTERS

The privileges granted to the Jews by Boleslaus, the leader of the Greater Poland, extended in their favor.

In the name of the Lord, amen. We, Casimir, by the grace of God, king of Poland, and also the lord and heir of Poznań of the lands of Krakow, Syradia, Sandomierz, Lancicia, and Cuiavia, wish to bring to the notice of the whole world, both present and future, that some of our Jews from the kingdom coming to the presence of our majesty and our nobles of the land having our abode in Greater Poland, offering a privilege given by the most serene leader Boleslaus in good memory, who was formerly the leader and lord of the lands of Poland, containing in himself the Jews themselves and their rights and statutes: which privilege indeed with the statutes of our royal majesty and the providence of our lords and nobles weighing with mature deliberation, we read the series of the said privilege word for word, and finding nothing in it that displeased our majesty or seemed to derogate in any way from the law: having regard to this, we ordered and adhered to renew the said privilege and to confirm, establishing that it is acceptable, acceptable, and firm.

First of all, we decree that for money, movable or immovable property of any kind, or for a criminal cause affecting the person or property of the Jews, no Christian shall act against the Jews for any movable or immovable property touching, as it is preferred, the life or goods of the Jews themselves, such A Christian against the aforesaid Jews, if he accuses any one of any matter, even of a criminal, is not admitted to testify, except with two good Christians and two good Jews, who all the above-mentioned are not infamous in their humanity; but since they are accepted, if the aforesaid Christian has convicted any of the Jews, then that Jew must first be punished for what the aforesaid Christian has slandered or blamed. Those two Christians must swear on the holy Cross, namely thus: So help us God and the holy Cross, etc. according to the custom of the Christians themselves; The Jews, however, will swear on the rodal ten preceptors according to the custom of the Jews themselves, on the sum of which will extend to fifty marks cast of pure silver; and if it were lower than the aforesaid sum of fifty marks of silver, then the Jews themselves will have to swear on the fern, or kolcze, around the school hanging in the door, according to their custom, this is in such a way or the wheel: So help us God who enlightens and darkens and the books of Moses; This is how the oath of the

Jews must be made, and not otherwise, for any matter, be it great or small, by keeping the oath, and this must be commanded by the minister, or otherwise by the wozni or skolni, to whom it is demanded.

Likewise, if any one of the Christians hinders a Jew, asserting that he has invaded his pledges, and the Jew denies this: then if the Christian himself refuses to accept the faith of the Jew by a simple word, the Jew must be free from him by swearing without the Christian.

Furthermore, if a Christian has pledged a pledge or pledge for a smaller sum of money, and the Jew, saying, asserts that it will be a larger sum, then the Jew (sic), having taken an oath to himself according to their custom, such a Christian will have to pay the Jew to him and will be bound to pay the principal sum of money, together with usury without all to give procrastination.

Moreover, the Jew will be able to receive all the pledges that have been offered to him, by whatever name they are called, with the exception of blood-soaked or wet ones, and sacred vestments dedicated to divine worship, which he will by no means accept. I suppose that he would give the same to some presbyter to keep, because he cannot keep it alone.

Likewise, if any Christian hinders a Jew because of a pledge which the Jew has, which has been stolen from him by violence, the Jew shall swear on the pledge at that time and say: when such a pledge or pledge was invaded upon me, I did not know that it had been stolen away or stolen by violence, but I believed the pledge would be just and free. A Jew will swear by his oath, how much is a pledge of this kind invaded for him; and thus, to the Jew, having been purged, the Christian himself will have to pay to him the principal money in which such pledge is bound, and the interest accruing from the time of the obligation, in reality and with effect.

Likewise, if by chance a fire occurs by chance, or if the property and goods of a Jew together with some of the pledges are stolen by stealth, then the aforesaid

Jew must protest with the testimony of some of the Jews who are his neighbors, that the property or goods together with the pledges stolen from him were stolen from him and received and by no means a Christian willing to have such pledges invaded, but a Jew, having taken an oath according to the custom of the Jews themselves, shall be free and released by the Christian himself. And if such a Jew does not presume to swear, then he shall be bound to add to the Christian himself as much as he had previously given on the forfeited pledge, and he shall be free from the Christian himself.

Likewise, if the Jews commit a de facto discord between themselves, or some kind of war, or a Jew with a Christian, and while thus contending they strike or wound each other, then neither the judge of the city, nor the consuls, nor any of the people, but only the palatine of the Jews themselves, or he who presides over them in his stead let him judge, and they will judge in such a way in the judgment, placing the stool with the Jews.

But if the aforesaid Jew, thus contending with any of the aforesaid men, has demanded that such a case be transferred to our majesty, then the palatine, or even the judge replaced by him, whosoever may be for the time being, shall bring such case of the Jew himself to us. And indeed, whatever cause should arise before the palatine between the Jews and the palatine or his substitute, if they have demanded it, must be brought before the arrival of our majesty.

Likewise, no palatine or captain ought to receive any proceeds, other poplathky, and contributions, dany, from the Jews, unless the Jews themselves have donated them of their own free will; and this because we reserve them for our treasure.

And we have also decreed that whatever cause arose because of discord or contention among the Jews, no one but their elders should judge this, provided that if they themselves were unable to discover the truth among them, they should then refer it to the lord palatine.

Likewise, if any of the Jews were not obedient to their superiors, from then on, such a one would pay the lord palatine a penalty of three marks, and his superiors likewise a penalty of three marks.

Moreover, if a Christian contends with a Jew in any way at the same time, and if the same Christian wounds a Jew with a bloody or bruised wound, or slaps him in the face, or knocks his hair from his head, then we give the same jurisdiction to the Jew himself: according to the custom upon the chain, otherwise known as the kolcze, at the door of the school of the Jews themselves, then such a Christian, if he has been sworn by a Jew, must and will be bound to give to the same Jew five marks for the cheek from each finger, ten marks from a bruised wound, and from a bloody wound half of his property, both movable and immovable, of the aforesaid Jew; but we reserve the remaining half of such goods for ourselves and our successors and for the palatine of this district, and we will decide otherwise according to our will. But for the hairs taken from the head of the Jew, the aforesaid Christian shall be bound to pay according to the decree of the lords in the presiding judgment, according to the position of the law.

Moreover, if a Christian has killed any of the Jews, then the Jew nearest to the slain Jew has perjured the Christian himself over the rodal ten preceptors according to the custom of the Jews, then we will and decree that such a Christian who has thus perjured himself through a Jew must be put to death, taxing him head for head; and it should not be done otherwise in that matter.

But if such a Christian, if he kills a Jew, somehow escapes, so that he cannot be captured or held in his hands, then whatever movable and immovable goods the Christian himself has, the first half of the said goods and inheritance must be handed over to the next of kin of the Jew, and the remaining half it must belong to our royal chamber.

Likewise, if such a fugitive of an interrupted Jew wishes to have safe employment, it must not be given to him, except with the consent of the said relatives of the interrupted Jew himself. Again, we will and decree: if any of the

Jews should enter the house of a Christian, no Christian should cause him any hindrance, burden, or trouble.

Likewise, every Jew may freely and safely go, cross or ride without any hindrance or arrest from city to city, from one province to another in our kingdom, according to the custom of secure freedom, without hindrance and arrest in all our cities and their subjects or provinces. And every Jew in our kingdom may freely and safely, without any hindrance, take with him his goods and goods or goods whatever he may or may have, sell them and buy others, exchange them and convert them to his own uses, and stay freely in the place of the city or town. and safely without any hindrance or arrest as long as it was convenient for him. In all the states, towns, villages, and other places of our kingdom, our king is to give every one of them security and safe rent, paying the usual tolls as other Christians pay, and not otherwise.

But if it happens to the Jews themselves, according to their custom, to take a dead Jew or Judean woman from one city to another city or province, then the publican of the place shall not dare to demand any such tolls from such a dead Jew. And if any of the tax-collectors, contrary to our established statutes and orders, has received the toll from such a dead Jew, then we decree and will that such a tax-collector must be judged as a thief, a robber, and a robber, and his goods, whatever they may be, must be returned to us.

Likewise, we will and decree that any Jew may freely and safely enter the public baths of the city together with the Christians, and must pay nothing extra, except as other inhabitants of the city.

Moreover, wherever the Jews have abode in any city or town of our kingdom, they may slaughter them cattle and sheep for meat for their own benefit; and if any of the meats were not according to their will and agreement according to custom, then they can sell them as best they can, or it will appear to them.

Likewise, if any of the Christians of the Jewish cemetery, where their burial is, violently cast or removed the stones there, or in any way destroy other places in the said cemetery of theirs, he who has done such things, his property and possessions shall be rolled over our royal chamber; which we wish to be done and held firmly according to the jurisdiction given by us to the Jews themselves.

Likewise, if any of the Christians should recklessly and presumptuously have thrown over their schools, our palatine, their guardian, such a Christian shall be bound and obliged to pay two tons of pepper for such a penalty.

Likewise, if any Jew is summoned by their judge in the first and second time, and if he does not appear, for whatever reason he was summoned, he must pay for each turn, and he will be bound to his judge for one talent of pepper. If, however, the person cited does not appear to the third party, whatever thing he is cited for, he will lose and lose it by doing so.

Again, the judge of the Jews themselves must not promulgate any sentence, or pronounce or sentence, unless he has first obtained the special consent of the Jews themselves.

Likewise, the judge of the Jews does not have to judge any Jew in his own right, unless such a Jew has been cited with a summons by skolny, ministerial; then first the judge must judge the said Jew according to that for which he is cited.

And if any Christian should receive wounds, whatever they may be, on a Jew, then he must show them to the skolnemu of the Jews themselves, and even to the ministerial: and the judge himself must not judge or place the judgment in such a case elsewhere, except in the vicinity of the school of the Jews themselves, or even where the said Jews are, when consenting to their judge on both sides, let them choose or depute a suitable place for this purpose; and there if a Christian brings two Jews and two Christians: that the same Jew gave him wounds and brought them: then the Jew will have to pay them according to the earthly composition.

Moreover, if any pledge of any Christian has been secretly taken away and invaded among the Jews themselves, he must ask the elder of their school, and that elder of their school, under their own anathema, will demand among the Jews about such pledge, and the same servant of the school must do this with the knowledge of the elder of the Jew. and if any of the Jews denied such a pledge, which had been taken by stealth, before the servant of the school and the elder of the Jews, and afterwards if he was arrested by any of them, such a Jew shall lose all his money given on the pledge and shall owe to the lord palatine three marks as a penalty.

Likewise, we decide and wish to have this, that none of the Christians themselves should complain of any ransoms by force, whatever they may be, in the dwellings or in the houses of the Jews themselves, unless first one mark of pure gold is placed on the border of the enemy of the Jew himself, which the Jew himself must lift. Then the Christian himself first inquired about the said bailiff. And if any of the Christians, not paying attention to and not taking care of our statutes, enters violently into the house of a Jew, complaining of his belongings, whatever he does not put in gold, such a Christian must be judged as a robber and a robber.

Likewise, no Christian should cite any Jew to a spiritual trial in any way and for any matter; and by any summons, neither a Jew shall answer before a judge in a spiritual judgment, but such a Jew shall be summoned before his own palatine who was then for the time, and further the aforesaid palatine with our captain existing for the time shall be bound to defend, protect, and intercede the Jew himself from such summons of law spiritual.

Moreover, we decree that any Jew who has any pledge, whatever it may be and whatever its value, and has stood beyond the due limit of the invasion, otherwise by siathaka zasthawa wysthala (?), so that the Jew will not keep it because he will not stand, the aforesaid Jew must show such pledge and put acting in the presence of their palatine, or acting on his behalf, and afterwards the said Jew must warn the Christian by means of a ministerial pre-acted bail for exemption; and if the Christian himself fails to redeem it after the ministerial warning, the Jew himself can convert the aforesaid bail to his own uses wherever he pleases. Likewise, if the aforesaid Jew did not show the pledge previously made and sold as promised, then the Jew himself shall be bound to the lord palatine for a penalty of three marks.

Likewise, we decide and wish to have the special consent of our majesty, that any of our Jews can accommodate and register their money or goods to our nobles of the land, of whatever state or condition they may be, and to confirm their money with land, military, civil, praetorial, and exchequer books. And on the fords, they can accommodate their money, regardless of the value of such things; and the Jew himself will not have to receive any more of the usury from such pledges, except for one gross weekly from each mark, as long as such pledges have stood with the Jews themselves.

And if it should happen that one of our Jews admonishes any of his debtors in any way whatsoever, to whom the debtors themselves were bound, either by the bonds of letters with their seals or by the inscriptions of pre-written books: indeed we spared the Jews themselves, that they may settle their money on the ground over their own binding goods, seals and where the aforesaid debtors, as they have registered themselves, recklessly did not take care of the Jews, and for the pledges as they were obliged to make a full payment, we command you palatines, captains, burgraves, and your vicegerents and any other officials who are willing to have them for the time being, inasmuch as you cause our Jews themselves to serve the final completion of justice with our aforesaid terrigines, their debtors, ministers and your subjects, so for money received as well as for usury, and you will not do otherwise.

And if they proceed to the binding of the hereditary goods in our lands, and if they affect the ministers upon pledges, otherwise nacziz, by order of our king, the aforesaid and every one of you shall owe and be bound to provide our Jews with aid and support according to the form of the law, the same Jews from all their wrongs protecting and defending them, and binding them Jews to such goods as our countrymen.

But if any of the Jews have been entrapped by you and your subjects in any of the hereditary goods of our terrigenes, we have established and decreed that in whose terrigenes some of the Jews were entrapped, such our terrigena must place with the Jew sureties for the good possession, which the Jew himself has accepted, of that district in which his goods are situated: that such a Jew of ours may hold and possess the same hereditary goods peacefully and quietly without the interference of any man, under such a condition that even the hereditary goods had jurisdiction, without any diminishment of right or dominion therein.

And if it should happen that one of our natives, whose hereditary goods some one of the Jews has held by real introgression, and the same native has not taken care to redeem the same goods at the lapse of years according to the terrestrial custom of antiquity, we decree that after the lapse of three years, the Jew himself may to freely sell the aforesaid hereditary goods, and to convert them to their own uses, as it seems to them better and more profitable to expedient.

And we have also decreed that whoever is a Jew who holds hereditary goods by indenture, shall not be obliged to ride for the expedition, nor to give anything for the expedition; and this because the Jews themselves are our treasurers.

Moreover, we decree that if any one of our people, be it a noble citizen or citizen, should be held by the aforesaid Jews for any sum of money on account of the obligation or the registration of the books, or in any way, and if it should happen that he himself should die, and his children should survive who were not yet of age, the same children of the aforesaid Jews They will not have to escape their childish years, but they must help the same Jews according to their obligations. and this because the Jews themselves ought to be made ready with their money for our needs as our subjects.

Likewise, if it happens that any of the Christians bring a child or a youth to any of the Jews, as is the custom of stealing, without the knowledge of the Jews themselves, such a Christian, whoever he may be, shall be punished in no other way than as another thief.

Likewise, we decree that no Jew should be blamed by any Christian for such a matter, saying that the Jews themselves of necessity used the blood of Christians annually, or the Sacraments of the Christian church: from which the statutes of Pope Innocent and the constitutions teach us that in such matters they do not they are guilty, because this is against their law. And if any Christian further by his rashness, otherwise upornosczia, blames any Jew for such things, otherwise obvynyelby, then we give and grant them such a right: that if such a Christian wants to bring and prove and end this matter of his, then he must prove to the three Jews good and possessions in our kingdom, who were not infamous in their humanity and were immovable in faith, and four Christians who were also well possessed in our kingdom and in their humanity not infamous and immovable in faith, otherwise nyeporusscheny; and if a Christian proves against a Jew by this kind of testimony, then the Jew himself shall be guilty of death and shall be punished. And as long as the Christian has not brought this kind of testimony and has not been able to prove it against the Jew, then he alone will be condemned to the same death with which the Jew should have been condemned. And if for such things our nobles of the land, or the citizens of our kingdom, have done violence to our Jews themselves, and I have not conquered them by right, then their goods must be turned over to our royal chamber, and they must be strained for our special grace.

And if any of our citizens of our kingdom cite any Jew, we decree this also, that the aforesaid Jew is not bound to answer before any judge, except before the palatine who was for the time being, and not elsewhere.

Even if it happens that some of our Christians want to redeem their hostages from any of the Jews who have been invaded, on their own Jewish holiday, the Sabbath, or on some of their own festivals, on which holidays the Jews themselves would not have dared to touch the money for the ransom, and to take the same money, and the Christian , not caring for such a festival of theirs, whatever it may be, wanting to retake his bail recklessly and by violence by breaking into the dwellings of the Jews themselves and taking away the aforesaid bail: such a Christian ought not to be judged in any other way than as a robber and a thief, as the jurisdiction demands over a thief and a robber.

Likewise, they can place their money on horses or other livestock, but only on the day around the evident evidence; but they do not accommodate at nighttime.

Furthermore, we decree and decree that if any of the Jews are accused by any of the Christians or any of them for any counterfeit money or theft, or for any small or great mischief that touches their throats and goods, such a Jew should not be taken captive by any of our dignitaries in the kingdom, nor to be judged, except by the palatine of the Jews themselves, or by his vicegerent; And for all the articles for which he has been accused, the Jew will be nearer to clearing himself of such infamy, taking with him some other Jews as witnesses, against him who accused the aforesaid Jew. And therefore, for all the fines which the Christians themselves would play, the Jew and the palatine will have to pay like terrigenes according to earthly custom, because we left our said Jews about the noble rights of our terrigenes.

Moreover, if it should happen that one of the Jews should publicly cry out over the violence inflicted on him by any people at night time, and cry out over his Christian neighbors living with him in the same city, and such Christian neighbors, hearing the Jew himself cry out, would not defend him from such violence and help him , we set and decreed that all the property of those Christian neighbors, whatever they may be, must be turned over to our royal chamber, but theirs should be preserved by our grace.

Moreover, we decree that all the Jews residing in our kingdom may freely, safely and without any hindrance or arrest, buy, procure, and trade with them all merchandise and other things for sale, by whatever name they may be called, in the same manner as Christians exist in our kingdom. And if any of the Christians refused to make such promises to the Jews themselves, or in some way disturbed them in such transactions, he would do this against all our royal statutes, and incur our great indignation from thence.

Likewise, we decree that every merchant, whoever he may be, selling his goods in the annual market or the weekly market, must sell to a Christian as well as to a Jew. But if he did otherwise, and the Jews themselves complained, then their goods for sale must be received for us and for the palatine.

Raczanz, January 18, 1358

As an elected amicable arbiter, he settles the controversies that have arisen between the Semovite leader of Mazovia and John, bishop of Poznan, and confirms the privileges which they had given to the church of Poznan.

And in order that all the foregoing may obtain the strength of a perpetual firmness, to the present privilege is affixed our seal.

In the name of the Lord, amen. We Casimir, by the grace of God, king of Poland, and also of Krakow, Sandomierz, Syradia, Lancic, Cuyavia, Mazovia, Dobrinia, Pomorania, the true lord and heir of the duchies and lands, arbitrator and amicable composer through the preeminent Semovite leader of Mazovia and Warsaw, our beloved prince, from one, and the venerable father in Christ, Lord John the bishop, and his Chapter of Poznań, on the other side, over all the controversies, wrongs, and displeasures held between them up to now and arising, elected freely requested and accepted, commending them in perpetual memory, we make known both to the present and to the future, to whom it is expedient to be present according to the tenor of the whole , that wishing to make a friendly agreement between the same parties, we praise, pronounce, judge, define and amicably sum up and command, that the same parties, viz.. the leader, [...] the bishop and [...] the Chapter shall henceforth be good and charitable friends. Likewise, we praise, agree and command as above, that the same ... the leader must allow the tithes of the church of Poznań to rent in the villages of his land, aput good kmethons or peasants, where the tithes will stand. Likewise, we commend, recommend, and command that the said leader should show, instruct, and teach by letter to the bishop and chapter of Poznań that tithes should not be given in a manipulated way, but should be paid with a certain amount of money ; but if he could not prove the same, then he would complain of an amicable arrangement with regard to the said Bishop and Chapter of Poznan for the payment of such tithes: otherwise the same tithe would be paid by manipulation according to the ancient custom of the land. Likewise, we praise, pronounce and command as above, that kmethons or free peasants, not slaves, both ducal and episcopal and the church of Poznań, from the ducal villages to the villages of the bishop and the church of Poznań, and vice versa, on every feast of the Nativity of our Lord, for residence and residence to be done according to the custom of the kingdom of Poland, they will pass freely without any hindrance. Likewise, we commend and command as above, that the said leader must pay, to be held, eighty-eight marks of the usual currency to the aforesaid bishop of Poznań, on the feast of Pentecost which will be next after the given presence; and one hundred marks of the same usual currency to the same bishop and Chapter of Poznań for tithes of robbery and damages to others, on the feast of the Purification of the Holy Virgin Mary following the said feast of Pentecost, continuously and immediately, without any diminution or contradiction. Furthermore, we praise, declare, pronounce, define, summarize and command that the aforesaid leader preserves and holds inviolably and unshakably the privileges granted to the church of Poznań by his predecessors, by himself and by his brother Casimir, with all its clauses and articles.

And indeed all the privileges with all their clauses, graces, liberties, indulgences, and all the articles contained in them, as the lord of the said duke and bishop by feudal reason, pertaining to our majesty, concerning the special devotion which we have to the aforesaid church of the blessed Peter and Paul of Poznan, of which we are patrons, having received and accepted, we confirm, ratify and approve of our certain knowledge. In addition, we praise, pronounce, and command as above, that the oft-mentioned leader and bishop with the Chapter must firmly and inviolably observe our praise and pronouncement of this kind, and in no way by themselves or through any person, publicly or secretly, neither the leader himself by receiving or appealing, nor the bishop dares to conflict with the Chapter by means of excommunications. And if any part in someone does not want to keep, this is signified to us by the keeping part, and we promise to support, maintain, and must defend ourselves as a keeping and parenting one, as if it were just in its right. in no case, however, the party not keeping, three hundred marks of the gross number of Prague current in our kingdom to us, and the same part shall be bound to pay and be bound: what penalty shall he be bound to pay, whenever he presumes to violate and contravene: these, to which our seal is attached to the kingdom, by the testimony of the letters.

Done and given in the castle of Raczanz and in the residence of the lord bishop of Vladislav, in the year of the Lord one thousand three hundred and fifty-eight, on the 15th of February, at three o'clock, in the presence of the parsons of both parties and their consencien, in the presence of these our faithful and beloved: the venerable father in Christ, lord Mathias, bishop of Vladislav, the illustrious Duke Wladislaus of Cuyavia and Gnewcovia, our prince, Jascon Iura of Krakow, Przeczslao of Poznań, the castellan, Daczbogone of Mazovia, John of Lancicia, Alberto Cuyavia the palatine, Sbiluto the prefect, Borzislao the cantor, Sandzivogio the custodian of Wladislavia, Florian the chancellor of Lanciciens, Msczugio the huntsman of Krakow, Pelca Kosczelecz the curie of our marshal, and others worthy of trust as many nobles.

Written and given by the hand of Johannes de Busszka, notary of our court.

Cruszvicia, January 20, 1358

He allows John, bishop of Poznań, to lease the town of his church, called Ślesin, according to Teutonic law, and to establish a weekly market there.

In the name of the Lord, amen. He is worthy of the pious and honorable, so that he may be consoled by the favors of princes, who have merited well in themselves and in theirs. Accordingly, we, Casimir, king of Poland by the grace of God, and also the heir and lord of the lands of Krakow, Sandomierz, Syradi, Lancic, Cuyavia, and Pomerania, declare to all present and future to whom this writing has come to notice, that the comfort and progress of the cathedral church in Poznań of the blessed Peter and Paul embracing the diligence of the apostles, inclined therefore to the manifold petitions of the venerable father in Christ the Lord John, bishop of the aforesaid church, our beloved chaplain, that at least from us for the benevolence of this exhibition, he may rejoice in some measure comforted by the benefit of retribution, we have henceforth given and are giving of his inheritance and of his church called Slessino , situated in the land of Poland in the district of Konyn, a town or city to be newly leased by the law of the Theuthunic New Forum, which is commonly called Srzedske, imposing the name of the city in a similar way to Slessino; removing at the same time all and every Polonician right, which they were in the habit of obstructing or in any way disturbing the Theuthunic right itself. Moreover, we absolve and free forever all the citizens and individual inhabitants of the aforesaid city of Slessino, from all the judgments and jurisdictions of all the palatines, castellans, judges, sub-judges, ministers and any officials of our kingdom: so that before them or any of them, for all causes great and small , for example thefts, whether murders, arson, blood, mutilations of limbs, and all other things, shall be fully answerable to no one, except the citizens and inhabitants of the city of Slessino in the presence of their advocate through the lord himself . . . the bishop or his successors deputed; to the lord .. the bishop or before us; however, as long as he has been summoned by a letter sealed with our seal, then he will be bound to answer those who complain about him according to his Teuthunic right: willing and present deciding, that the same city and its inhabitants, according to the full Teuthunic right of the New Forum, should preferably rejoice and enjoy in perpetual times, as the same Teuthunic right in its own it is distinguished by appropriate clauses and articles. Therefore, by the special grace of our royal majesty, we have admitted the forum on the third day of each week in the separated town or city of Slessino, to be held continuously and in common and freely, without any contradiction being at rest. In witness whereof, and for fuller evidence, we have hereunto affixed our seal. Done in Cruszvicia of the blessed martyrs Sebastian and Fabian, in the year of the Lord one thousand three hundred and fifty-eight, in the presence of these witnesses, the noblemen Pazskone of Gneznensi, Laurence of Landes, Sandyvogio of Nakeliensi, Janussius of Bechoviensis of Castella, Stanislaus Kyvala the judge of Cuyaviensis, Preczslao the subagazone of Kalisiensis, and many others worthy of trust. Given by the hands of Florian, chancellor of Lancic.

Zneno, January 27, 1358

He agreed to the exchange of the town of Albert Palatine of Cuiavia, called Dobrzelewice, with the town of Jaroslai, the archbishop of Gnez, named Lutkowo.

In the name of the Lord, amen. When alienations, commutations, and any other contracts concluded before the great kings [...] cannot in any way obtain the strength of perpetuity, unless they are confirmed by the custody of letters and the amicable witnesses, accordingly we Casimir, king of Poland, and not lord and heir of the lands of Krakow, Sandomerie, Syradie, Lancicie, Cuyavie, and Pomerania, to the notice of all the worlds, as well as to the notice of the future, in the present series, that our noble and faithful man, Lord Albertus Palatine of Cuyavi, approaching to the presence of us and our barons, was not forced or compelled, or by any having been led astray by error, but with his own mature deliberation, sound in mind and body, his village called Dobryiowicze, situated near Kowale in the land of Cuyaviensi, with all right and dominion and all and every encumbrance, rents and revenues and other appurtenances pertaining to the same village, as in his gadis and limits is circumferentially distinct from the ancient one, reserving no right and dominion for himself and his successors for posterity, with the divine providence of the venerable father Lord Jaroslaw in Christ, the holy archbishop of the church of Gneznes, for his own town called Luthcowo, situated near Pacoscz, and for thirty and counting seven marks and a half of the Prague grosses prepared and already paid, forty-eight grosses in each mark, he exchanged, gave, and exchanged justly with the title of exchange; and none the less, having obtained for himself and his legitimate heirs the right patronage of the church in Pacoscz, founded in honor of the blessed James the apostle, which is connected with the same town of Luthcowo, by the said lord archbishop to consummate the account of the same exchange, giving and resigning the same lord Albertus to the aforesaid lord [...] archbishop and to his successors the corporeal property of the aforesaid town of Dobrzeiowycze to be perpetually held, held and irrevocably possessed, exchanged, sold and converted to his own uses, as he and his successors shall see fit to expedient. Upon which both sides humbly begged us, that we might condescend to confirm the same exchange and resignation, with the apposition of money and the addition of the right of patronage to the church, from the fullness of our royal power. We, however, being favorably inclined to their petitions, ratify the same exchange and resignation, with the addition of money and the addition of the right of patronage to the church in Pacoscz, in all its clauses expressed above of our certain knowledge and confirm the present written patronage: willing and deciding that the said village of Dobrzeiowycze is thus exchanged , e [...] ertate, which the rest of the towns of the church in memory enjoy otherwise nominally expressed in our privilege, should enjoy and rejoice forever.

In proof of which we have taken the fuller evidence of the present letter to confirm it under the protection of our seal. Done in Zneno on the next Sabbath after the Conversion in the year of the Lord one thousand three hundred and fifty-eight, in the presence of noble men, lords Matthias of Poznań, Iohannes of Lanciciensi palatine, [...]ico of Krakow and chancellor of Lanciciensi, Preczlao the castellan of Poznan, Dobeslao the judge, Andrea the butler of Calizensi, and Ian [...] odsky Given by the hand of Henry of Ruskowo, notary of the court of our majesty.

ROYAL POLISH LETTERS

Sneyno, January 28, 1358

Confirms the exchange of the inheritances of Hector of Łącko, called Łącko and Wilcze, with the inheritances of the monastery of Byszewo, namely Szpital górny, Zaduszniki, Glewo and Złotopole.

In the name of the Lord, amen. Since all the permutations and resignations are the more solid and the stronger, the more united and consummated, brought to the presence of the princes, marked by the testimony of the letters of the princes and perpetuated, therefore we Casimir, by the grace of God, king of Poland and Russia, and also of the lands of Krakow, Sandomierz, Syradia, and Lancicia , Mazovia, Dobrynie, Cuiavie and Pomerania, the true lord and heir, both to the present and to the future, we wish that this series of letters, by which it is convenient for inspection, should be known to all, that approaching the presence of our majesty and our barons, a reverend and religious man, brother John of the Cistercian Order, abbot of Byssovia, together with their assembly, on the one hand, and lord Hector de Lanczsco's heirs, on the other hand, our faithful and beloved, for the convenience and benefit of the proximity and contiguous contiguousness of their inheritances to each of them, acknowledged that they had made such an exchange of their inheritances, and in this manner and form: namely, that the same abbot with his congregation, purely by reason of exchange, from the said Lord Hector the inheritances and villages of Lanczsko Magnum with the right of patronage and Lanczsko Novum, commonly called Wilcze, with the lots belonging to the said inheritances, Ossec and Rusca and Czeligoscz, in the land of Nakl situated, for himself and his monastery and congregation, with all the benefits, fruits, and encumbrances of each, according to the fact that the same towns named above in their gads and borders are distinctly and boundedly receiving and accepting, their towns and their monastery, the Hospital of St. Gotthard with the New Hospital and with the right patronage, Zadusniki with the whole lake of Cuczino and the inflowing or outflowing rivers, Glevo, Slotopole situated in the land of Dobrinensi, with all the benefits, fruits, encumbrances, assessments and appurtenances of all in the land, waters and trees, now occupied and to be held in the future, as the same town in their possessions according to the distinction of boundaries, they are limited, to the said Lord Hector and his descendants and legitimate successors by right of inheritance for ever and ever to hold, possess, have, sell, exchange, give and convert as it pleases the said Lord Hector and his posterity, they surrendered no right and dominion for themselves having exchanged the same parts with the said towns, that is to say, the lord abbot and the convent, and the aforesaid lord Hector, reserving in every way: they humbly besought our majesty, that admitting the same exchange, we would deign to confirm it. We, on the other hand, nodding to their supplication and noting of course their benefit and comfort from the exchange itself, having the same exchange as having been reasonably made, acceptable and accepted, we approve, ratify and confirm those to whom our seal is affixed by the testimony of letters. They circumscribed the act in Sneyno on the Sunday in which it is sung, under the year of the Lord one thousand three hundred and fifty-eight, in the presence of these witnesses: the venerable father in Christ, Lord Jaroslaw, archbishop of Gnezdne, Maczcon of Poznań, John of Lancic, Albert of Brescens, the palatine Janussius of Krakow, Florian of Lancic, chancellors, Predborio the captain of Cuiavia, Ade the sub-chamberlain of Kalisiensi, and many other trustworthy men. Given by John of Busco, our majesty's notary.

Gnezda, January 29, 1358

The advocate of the city of Poznań sells John the Mint and establishes his rights.

In the name of the Lord, amen. For although the city took its name from the unity of the citizens, yet because of the diversity of men, times, and events, discord, dissensions, quarrels, mischief, and displeasure often arise among the citizens; to the tribunal, that according to the path of justice, quarrels, vices, and malice should be banished from the states and examined, and virtues, concord, and peace should be established and maintained. Accordingly, we Casimir, by the grace of God, king of Poland and Russia, and also the lord and heir of the lands of Krakow, Sandomierz, Syradie, Lancicia, Cuyavia, and Pomerania, commending to our perpetual memory both the present and the future, we make known by this series of letters to whom it is expedient for all, that we wish our city Poznan to be by rights and justice to the king and to be subject, I will summon ours there in Poznań and the third penny coming from the judgments, reserved to our two majesties, from the mere legality of our majesty, acceding to this counsel of our faithful barons, for one hundred and twenty marks of Prague gross, counting forty-eight gross marks for each, which we acknowledge that we have had in full and have been paid, we have sold and surrendered to the faithful and honest man John the Mint, a citizen of Poznań, and to his legitimate heirs, with the same title and account gratuitously, purely and purely by sale, we surrender, condescend, incorporate and assign, by right of inheritance from time to time to be held in perpetuity, to be possessed, to be held, to be sold, to be exchanged, to be given, and to be converted according to the discretion of John the Advocate of Poznań and his posterity, without prejudice to this agreement requested and obtained. Thus adding this, and declaring that the said John the Advocate and his posterity, in the said city of Poznan, shall preside over the judgment by name, and shall have the authority of our majesty, judging, sentencing, and determining all civil and criminal cases, according to the continence and form of the laws of Maydburg and of the statutes: of these to which the seals of our majesty are affixed as evidence of letters.

Acted in Gnezda on the second day after the Sunday in which it is sung, in the year of the Lord 1358, in the presence of these witnesses: Maczcone Borcovicz of Poznań, John of Lancic, Alberto Palatine of Brest, Preczslao of Castella, Nicholas the judge of Poznań, Wirbentha the captain of Poland, and many other trustworthy.

Given by the hand of Lord Otto, chancellor of Poland.

Lublin, June 7, 1358

Restored to the church of Gnezda the villages of Bąków, Złaków, Wyskieniec and Łaźniki.

In the name of the Lord, amen. Because it is the property of kings to render to each one what is his own, especially to the blessed mother Church, therefore we Casimir, by the grace of God, king of Poland, and also the true lord and heir of the lands and duchies of Krakow, Sandomierz, Syradie, Lancicia, Cuyavia, and Pomorania, both to the present and to the future of this series of letters we make it known to all: because we were informed by an evil and sinister suggestion, that the towns below, namely Bancovo, Prziczina, formerly named Gyzicze, part of the town of Slonovo, the church of Gnezn, Wizkidnicza, and the middle of Laznyki according to which it divides the path commonly called Karlova Droga, belonged to us. we had introverted ourselves from them; knowing, however, that they are and have been from ancient times, of which there is no record of the contrary, the archbishoprics and church of Gnezna, the same villages and any of them with all their products, revenues, assessments, uses, appurtenances, all pools, lakes, mills, forests, . . and devoutly, acceding to this by the sound and mature counsel of our barons, we return, restore, approve and incorporate, to hold, hold, possess, and convert to the pleasure and benefit of the church of Gnezn for perpetual times, with the same graces and liberties as the other goods of the said church of Gnezn privileged by our predecessors and by us, desiring and deciding to rejoice in every way, by the testimony of these letters to whom our royal seal is affixed. Done in Lublin on the eighth day of Corpus Christi, in the year of the Nativity of the same thousand, three hundred and fifty-eighth, in the presence of these witnesses: lords Daczbogone of Ploczen, John of Lancic, Albert Palatine of Brest, Wilczcon of Sandomierz, Eustace of Lublin, Zavissa of Sandeczen, Vito of Polanecz, Grothon of Zavichosten of Castilian, Otto of Poland, Hermannus Cuyavie to the chancellors, Peter Neorza the tribune of Krakow, Raphael the sub-chamberlain of Sandomierz, and many other trustworthy witnesses. Given by the hand of Lord Florian, chancellor of Lancic, written by John de Busco, chaplain and notary of our majesty.

Krakow, June 25, 1358

Archbishop Jaroslaw of Gneznes. He acquitted him of the impeachment which Semovitus, the leader of Mazovia, had raised over certain immunities of the people of the church of Gneznens, in the district of Łowicz.

We, Casimir, by the grace of God, king of Poland, wish to convey to all the news this series of letters: that when, through the most serene prince, Lord Semovite, the illustrious leader of Mazovia, the actor, over certain rights inscribed below to the venerable Lord Yaroslaus, the father in Christ, divine providence moved the archbishop of the holy church of Gnezn, as a defendant would have been the subject of the question before us, because it was said on the part of the said duke, that the kmethones, the inhabitants and men of the district of Lovice, were bound to do and pay for the same every service and rural labor of the duke himself; The districts of Lovica are bound to give exactions to themselves, so that they are held to be bound for the hire of game and other things. And although Lord Iaroslaus, the aforesaid archbishop, had been absent from arduous business, hindered by himself and his church, so that he could hardly appear within the limits so short, for the delay of which he requested that Lord Semovitus, the duke already mentioned, extend the aforesaid limit to the day of blessed Martin: our messengers certain, namely Boguslau of Lucawa, then we ordered Stanislaus the castellan of Malogosten to be appointed, to whom the aforesaid leader would not consent to delay: and notwithstanding this, for the experience of the aforesaid rights, a peremptory term was given and assigned, by one edict for the tribes, through our faithful master, John Jura, the castellan of Krakow, on the morrow at the feasts of St. John the Baptist. When the term arrived, reverencing the aforesaid Lord Jaroslav the archbishop in Christ, appearing legitimately in his own name and in his church of Gnezna, and accusing the aforesaid leader of his disobedience, the same leader did not take care to comply legitimately in the term prefixed to him, neither by himself nor by a representative. As for us, at that time, in the judgment of the presidents with our faithful, through our barons, that is to say, Andreas the sub-chamberlain of Krakow and many others, the aforesaid lord archbishop and his church, as far as the aforesaid rights for which he was sued, stood justified and absolved from the duke his own impeachment, constantly demanding justice. Ratifying and approving the opinion of our faithful then duly promulgated, we confirm with those present; in witness whereof, we have made the present scribe, strengthened with the seal of our seal.

Done at Krakow on Monday, the morrow of St. John the Baptist, under the year of the Lord, *1359*. Eighthly, in the presence of these witnesses: Immramus palatine, Andrew the aforesaid sub-chamberlain of Krakow, John the dean of decrees, the chancellor of Krakow, Florian Lancicius, Andrew the subjudge of Krakow, Marcus the custodian of Sandomiria, and many others.

Glovna, January 20, 1359

Confirms the privileges which they had given to the monastery of Łekno.

In the name of the Lord, amen. We Casimir, by the grace of God, king of Poland, as well as lord and heir of the lands of Krakow, Sandomierz, Syradia, Lancicia, Cuiavia, and Pomerania, make it known to those who are expedient for all that the religious man Brother Hermannus, abbot of the monastery of Lukna, having come to our presence with his assembly of the Cistercian Order, begged humbly and devoutly, that we would deign to confirm the privileges given, granted and donated by our royal majesty over certain goods of the monastery itself, by the illustrious princes, that is to say, Wladyslaw and Boleslaus, the leaders of Poland.

But we, nodding favorably to the just supplications of the abbot himself, graciously confirm the aforesaid privileges with their clauses and articles in the tenor of their content, giving to the abbot and his congregation this letter of ours, secured by our seal, as a strength and testimony of perpetual firmness. Done at Glovna on the day of the blessed martyrs Sebastian and Fabian, in the year of the Lord 1359, in the presence of: Preczslao of Poznań, Andrea of Kalissia, Vincencio of Sremen of Castilian, Adam the sub-chamberlain of Kalissia, Virzbanta our captain of Poland and Lord Florian our chancellor of Lancic, and several other trustworthy.

Czanszim, January 28, 1359

Grants to Bishop John of Poznań to lease a city in the bottom of the town of Dolsk by right of the New Market, and to be able to establish a weekly market in the same.

In the name of the Lord, amen. When it is requested that there is no doubt that it is just, the mind of princes must not be undeservedly inclined to listen to it. Therefore let both the present age and the future know that we Casimir, by the grace of God, king of Poland, and also the lord and heir of the lands of Krakow, Sandomierz, Syradia, Lancicia, Cuyavia, and Pomerania, considering the just petitions of the venerable father John in Christ, the divine and apostolic see of the bishop of Poznań church, our beloved chaplains, and of course noting that the Teutonic and civil law brings us and our kingdoms many benefits and multiplies the advantages of the subjects, we grant to the same lord John the bishop to lease the city according to the Teutonic law of the New Forum, which is commonly called Szredske, at the bottom of his town of Dolsco, itself from now on calling the city by the same name Dolsco, with all the rights, articles, points and clauses of the same Teutonic law, permanently obtained and inviolably observed in the same city. Let us remove and completely exclude there all the Polonician rights, savages, manners and customs, all the anxieties and pre-anxieties which used to hinder the very Teutonic law. Moreover, we decree that the market of all things for sale in the same city shall be celebrated on Wednesdays every week at perpetual times. Moreover, we decree and completely release the advocate and citizens of the mentioned city of Dolsco from all judgments and jurisdictions of all palatines, castellans and any judges and officials of our kingdom; so that before them or any of theirs, for causes great and small, capital and criminal, for instance theft, blood, murder, arson, and all other things, they ought not to answer to anyone who complains about them at all, except the citizens before their advocate according to the aforesaid Teutonic law. But he is not otherwise advocated, except only before his aforesaid lord bishop or his successors, and when he is cited by the letter of the lord bishop himself, he will answer those who complain about him in no other way than by his Teutonic law. In testimony of all of which we have given the present letter, strengthened with the seal of our seal. Done at Czanszim on the eighth day of Saint Agnes the Virgin, in the ninth year of the Lord *1359*, in the presence of these witnesses: Otto, chancellor of Poland and prefect of Gneznen, Paszcon of Gneznen, Vincentius of Sremen, the castellan of Sremen, Nicholas the hunter of Gneznen, Hamleto the subagazone, Andrea Dobeslavicz, and many other trustworthy.

Given by the hands of the Chancellor.

Crusvicie, February 6, 1359

Borzislav grants to the abbot of Mogilno that he can rent the forest of his monastery called Neboz in the village and grants his kmeton freedom from all payments and royal collections for less than twenty consecutive years.

Let them all know that they will have notice that we, Casimir, king of Poland, by the grace of God, from the office of God granted to us the benefits of our kingdom from the forests and forests, from which no benefit came to us, are desiring to expand more widely and to increase incessantly, and that by the help of the density of the forests discovered, with the grace and power of freedom, he will be reformed, and considering the just requests of the religious man brother Borzislai, abbot of Mogylno, so that he can rent the forest called Neboz vulgarly and the merica or gage around their village Woyuczino, located in the territory of Czbari, and convert it to better uses, for each and every kmethon in the forest and merica aforesaid to be leased and leased, from the present date below for twenty consecutive years from all payments and collections to our royals, namely from pigs, from cows, from oxen, from poradlne, from fences, from expeditions, and in general from all taxes, wherever to be called by name, we give and grant full and complete liberty to those to whom our seal is affixed by the testimony of letters. Given at Crucifixion on the day of the blessed Virgin Dorothea, in the ninth year of the Lord 1359.

February 9, 1359

Grants to Albert Palatine and Hector the Sub-pincerna of Bresteni, the brothers, that they may lease their town of Pakość into a city by Teutonic law.

In the name of the Lord, amen. It is worthy that the well-deserved prizes should be emphasized. Therefore, let both the present age and the future know that we, Casimir, by the grace of God, are king of Poland, and also lord and heir of the lands of Krakow, Sandomierz, Syradie, Lancicia, Cuyavia, and Pomerania, in consideration of the faithful and trustworthy services and just petitions of our faithful Albertus Palatine and Hector the sub-pinch of Breston. brothers, and of course noting that the Teutonic and civil law brings much benefit to us and our kingdoms, we grant to the same brothers Albert and Hector to lease a city by Teutonic law, which our city Wladislavia Juvenis enjoys, situated at the bottom of his town of Pakoscz in the land of Cuyaviens, the very city of the same name By naming Pakoscz from now on, all the rights, articles and clauses of the same Teutonic law in the same city are permanently obtained and observed. Let us also remove and completely exclude there all the Polish rights, services, manners and customs, all the anxieties and burdens, which used to hinder or disturb the Teutonic (right) itself. We decree, moreover, that the market of any kind of things for sale shall be celebrated in the same city on the second day of every week at perpetual times. Moreover, we absolve and completely free the aforesaid brothers Albertus and Hector, advocates and citizens or inhabitants of the mentioned city, from all judgments, jurisdictions and powers of all palatines, castellans and any judges and officials of our kingdom; so that before them or any of them, for causes great and small, capital and criminal, such as theft, bloodshed, murder, arson, and all other things, they ought to answer to no one at all, except the citizens before their lawyer by Teutonic law, and the lawyer before his aforesaid masters and to their successors, indeed the lords themselves and their successors before us or our general judge, as long as they have been summoned by a letter sealed with our seal and the lawyer himself has been summoned as necessary, then they are bound by law to answer those who complain about themselves. In witness whereof, our seal is hereunto affixed. Done at Brest on the eighth day of the glorious Purification of the holy Virgin Mary, in the year of the Lord one thousand three hundred and fifty-ninth, in the presence of these witnesses: Chebda palatine of Syradi, Dobeslao of Crusficia, Pascon of Brest, Woyslao of Bidgostien of Castilian, Stanislao of Cuyaviene, judge, and Florian of Lancic, chancellor, and several other trustworthy persons. Written by Nicolaus Bohemus, notary of our court, a canon of the church of Vislice, on the command of Lord Florian, chancellor of Lancius aforesaid.

Brest, February 12, 1359

He exchanges the inheritances of Cień and Michałowice with the inheritances of the church of Gnezna, namely Chrościce, Królowice and Czarków, and also allows the archbishop to be able to buy possessions in the kingdom of Poland for four hundred marks.

In the name of the Lord, amen. In order that the actions or deeds of mortals, which are done and ordered in time, may not pass away and waver in the course of time, it is necessary that they be brought back to perpetual memory by the protection of letters and the annotation of witnesses. Therefore let both the present age and the future know that we, Casimir, by the grace of God, king of Poland, and also lord and heir of the lands of Krakow, Sandomierz, Syradie, Lancicia, Cuyavia, and Pomerania, by the early deliberation and common counsel of our barons, have come to this, the exchange of our royal goods with reverently in Christ the father lord Jaroslav, the divine providence of the holy church of Gneznes, the archbishop, we have done in this way: that with the aforesaid inheritances of the Gneznes underwritten, namely Chroslina and Crolevicze in the lands of Krakow and Sandomirie situated near Wislicia, with the tenths of each, and also Czarnkow before Conyn in the land of Poland, without tithes, with the rents and revenues pertaining to the same inheritances as they are distinctly circumferentially in their borders, received for us and our kingdom in the manner and name of exchange, appropriated and permanently incorporated, lord Jaroslaw the archbishop and his church of Gneznen our inheritances Czena and Michalow in the land of Poland situated near Kalis, with all the benefits, rents, bors, and all the proceeds pertaining to the same inheritances limited as they are within their borders, and with all the right and dominion as we alone held, we have given, assigned, inscribed, incorporated nothing for ourselves fully reserving in the same and we give by the present right of inheritance to be held, held, given, sold, possessed and converted by the will of the Lord Archbishop Jaroslav himself and his successors to the church of Gnezna. Moreover, we confirm to the said lord archbishop and to all his descendants the church of Gnezn, the mill in Queczyssow, which once belonged to the nuns of Strzelno, which was duly withdrawn from the same nuns by way of sale, in perpetuity and hereditary possession, imposing perpetual silence on the aforesaid nuns for the same mill. Moreover, by our special grace, we have admitted to the aforesaid lord Jaroslaw the archbishop, and we admit by presents, to buy and procure goods and possessions for four hundred marks gross in our kingdom, wherever it pleases his will. And the goods and possessions of the aforesaid Czena and Michalow, and all others for the aforesaid money of four hundred marks to be procured by the lord archbishop himself, must be free and absolutely from all our royal payments, that is to say, from a pig, a cow, an ox, a poral, a stan, from Stroza, from Przewod, from labors, and any other collected, torts and pretenses, both general and particular, by whatever Polish term they may be called. In testimony and fuller evidence of all of them, we have caused the present letter to be given, marked with the protection of our great seal. Given and performed at Brest on the third week next after the eighth of the Purification of the holy Virgin Mary, in the year of the Lord one thousand three hundred and fifty-ninth, in the presence of these witnesses: Daczbogon of Plocen, Albert of Cuyavien, John of Lancicien palatine, Pascon of Gneznen, Chebda of Syradiensi Castilian, Wyrzbantha captain of Poland, and others many trustworthy. Given by the hand of Lord Florian, chancellor of Lancic, written by the hand of Pribislai, canon of Gneza, and prefect of the churches of Sandomierz.

Lovicz, February 13, 1359

Confirms the letters which he had given to Jaroslaw the archbishop of Gneznes

In the name of the Lord, amen. Because those things which are done and contracted before the captains and officials of the kings, are approved and authorized by the kings and princes by merit, and therefore we Casimir, by the grace of God, king of Poland, and also of the duchies and lands of Krakow, Sandomierz, Syradia, Lancicia, Cuyavia, and Pomorania, the true lord and heir forever commemorating the tenor of these letters, we make it known to whom it is expedient for all, that approaching the presence of us and our barons, the reverend father Lord Jaroslav, archbishop of the church of Saint Gnezdne in Christ, our beloved prince, a certain instrument with the seal of Lord Wirzbanthe, our captain of Poland, not abolished, not shaved, nor in some part of himself he showed the suspect before us and exhibited it for us to read.

Having read this instrument, the said lord archbishop humbly begged us that we would approve the same instrument. We, on the other hand, nodding more generously to his just prayers, confirming, authorizing and ratifying the aforesaid instrument with all its articles and clauses, we appropriate, inscribe and incorporate the aforesaid title of the aforesaid exchange, to the aforesaid lord archbishop, to his successors and to the holy church of Gnezdnes, from our sure knowledge; determining that the same rights, graces, exemptions and liberties, which the rest of the church of the town of Gnezdne are privileged by us or our predecessors, to enjoy completely and rejoice: these to which the seal of our majesty is attached by the testimony of letters. Done at Lovicz on the Wednesday after the day of Blessed Scholastica, in the year of the Lord one thousand three hundred and fifty-ninth, in the presence of: Chebda palatine of Syradien, Florian chancellor of Lancic, Nynota of Radomien, Zemacus of Wissegroden of Castilian, Pelca marshal, Thomcon canon of Krakow of our familiar curia, with many other faithful witnesses, worthy Given and written by John de Busco, chaplain and notary of our majesty.

Krakow, June 11, 1359

To Jaroslav, the archbishop of Gneznes, for a hundred gross marks, in the name of the tenth quadrennial, he gives apocha received by the same and the clergy of his diocese.

We, Casimir, by the grace of God, king of Poland, acknowledge that in this series of letters, which are expedient for all, from the venerable Lord Jaroslaw, the divine providence in Christ, the father, the archbishop of the holy church of Gnesden, and his chapter of the same church, and also from the clergy of his diocese, he received one hundred marks of gross for the last term of the fourteenth year of the quadrennial , of which we absolve the lord archbishop himself, his aforesaid chapter, and the clergy of his diocese with a sum of money, and leave. Moreover, of our special grace, of the aforesaid one hundred marks of gross, we gave fifty marks of gross in the name of the Ruthenian War, and we gave the remaining fifty marks of gross for our royal chapel in the church of Gnesdens and did not fail to assign it. In witness whereof we have hereunto affixed our seal.

Done and given at Krakow on the third day after the feast of Pentecost, in the year of the Lord 1359.

Krakow, October 3, 1359

Confirms the sale of the inheritance of Jerzowice, made by the heirs of Bieganów into the property of the church of Gnezna.

In the name of the Lord, amen. Since all sales, resignations, and renunciations proceeding under the approval of the princes, let them rejoice the more in the firmness with which they were written with the same authentic strength, therefore we Casimir, by the grace of God, king of Poland, as well as of Krakow, Sandomierz, Syradie, Lancicia, Cuiavia, and Pomorania, the true lord and heir of the lands, known We make, both present and future, a series of these letters, which are expedient for all, that coming to the presence of us and our barons, our faithful Thomislav, son of Woyslay, Nicolaus son of Gethcze, and the lady Sventoslava left behind by Imislai, the heirs of Beganow, being sane and reasonable, not coerced, not compelled, not surrounded by deceit or fraud, but with the good and mature will of their ancients, they publicly recognized and were acknowledged and confessed, the part and parts of the inheritance of Jezovicze named, situated near Curzelow, themselves and theirs any contingent and contingent, as the same parts of theirs the whole same they contain the heritage of Jezovicze, as it is in its gads and borders from the ancient circumferentially distinct and bounded, with all the benefits, fruits, assessments, rents, appendages and burdens to each and all, which are now and may be in the future, for ten and one hundred marks gross The number of Praguers current in our kingdom, that is to say, counting forty-eight gross for each mark, reverently in Christ the father Lord Jaroslav, the archbishop of the holy church of Gneznes, and that he sold himself to the same church of Gneznes; each of them relinquishing his part of the inheritance freely to the aforesaid lord archbishop and his church of Gneznes, to be held, held, possessed, and converted and disposed of according to his pleasure in perpetuity, reserving no right or dominion to himself or to his children or to any successors therein; expressly promising for all eviction, intercession and excommunication, in court or out of court, if by any one or some of the aforesaid lord, the archbishop and the church of Gneznen, a question or any hindrance should arise and take place. We, therefore, the aforesaid sales and resignations, as having been rightly and rationally and for pious purposes entered into and celebrated, out of reverence for the blessed Adalbert the martyr and glorious pontiff, the said church of Gnezna and our patron, graciously and most devoutly accepting and willing to have them firm and perpetual, by the Lord himself to the archbishop, to his successors, and to the church of Gneznes, we appropriate, attribute, inscribe and incorporate, declaring and decreeing: henceforth the same inheritance of Jezovicze with all its inhabitants, in all things and entirely, to enjoy and rejoice in the same graces, benefits and liberties, with which all other inheritances of the church of Gneznes they are privileged and fortified by the grant of us and of our progenitors and predecessors: to whom the seal of our majesty is affixed by the testimony of letters.

Done at Krakow on the Thursday next after the feast of the blessed Michael the Archangel, in the year of the Lord one thousand three hundred and fifty-ninth, in the presence of Imram palatine of Krakow, Dobeslaus castellan of Vislic, Nicholas called Puscz subdapifer, Wylczkone sub-judicator of Sandomierians, James heir of Cluczsko and Dominic chamberlain of the said palatine.

Given by the hands of Janussius, our chancellor of Krakow.

Krakow, January 6, 1360

He has approved the resignation of the town of Komparzew from Peter de Bogorja to the Gneznensi church under the same conditions as himself.

In the name of the Lord, amen. Since all the resignations and renunciations proceeding under the consent of the princes, let them rejoice the more in the firmness with which they have been written with the same authentic strength, therefore we Casimir, by the grace of God, king of Poland, as well as of Krakow, Sandomierz, Sirade, Lancicie, Cuyavia, and Pomeranian duchies, and the true lord and heir of the lands, forever commemorating these to whom it is expedient both for the present and for the future, we make it known to all by the testimony of letters, that our faithful Peter of Bogoria, coming to the presence of us and our barons, being sound in all things and rational, not forced nor surrounded or seduced by any trick, but with good and mature deliberation renouncing the town of Camperzevo, which is said to be situated near Curzelov, he surrendered it to Christ the Father Lord Jaroslaw, to the holy church of Gneznes, the archbishop of Gneznes, and to the same church of Gneznes, leaving no right, property or dominion to himself or to his heirs or successors in any way whatsoever, with the same conditions and methods in which he had bought it the village, in a certain inscribed instrument which he produced in our medium, with contents, expressed and more clearly specified.

But we the aforesaid king, of course, considering that as all things are of God Almighty and proceeded from him, so they should lawfully enter into the Church in the person of the holy mother militant, the aforesaid sale of the Camparzevo inheritance and the resignation made to the aforesaid Peter of Bogoria, with all the means, clauses, by the articles and conditions held and declared in the aforesaid instrument to the aforesaid Lord Archbishop of Gneznes and the same church of Gneznes, we fully approve, ratify and confirm the inheritance of Camparzevo with all its encumbrances, appurtenances and interests, held and having, as already said We attribute, ascribe, appropriate and incorporate to the lord archbishop and his church of Gneznes and their successors for perpetual times to have, to possess and to dispose and convert at their pleasure; declaring the same heritage of Camparzevo with all its inhabitants, to enjoy and rejoice in the same graces and liberties, with which all the other heritages of the church of Gnezna, as you prefaced, are privileged and protected by the grant of us and our predecessors: these to which the seal of our majesty is affixed with the testimony of letters. Done at Krakow on the eighth day of Saint John the Apostle and Evangelist, in the year of the Lord one thousand three hundred and sixtieth; in the presence of Iaskone Jura of Krakow, Iaskone of Woynice, Ninot of Radomien, Savissa of Sandeczeni Castilian, Peter called Neorza tribune, Niczcone called Puscz subdapifer to the Krakowians, and Otto the chancellor of Poland. Given by the hands of the venerable Janussius, doctor of decrees, our chancellor of Krakow and dean.

The Scriptorium Project is the work of a small group of lay people of various apostolic churches who are interested in the preservation, transmission, and translation of the works of the early and medieval church. Our efforts are to make the works of the church fathers accessible to anyone who might have an interest in Christian antiquities and the theological, philosophical, and moral writings that have become the bedrock of Western Civilization.

To-date, our releases have pulled from the Greek, Syriac, Georgian, Latin, Celtic, Ethiopian, and Coptic traditions of Christianity, and have been pulled from sundry local traditions and languages.

The Scriptorium Project is the work of a small group of lay people of various apostolic churches who are interested in the preservation, transmission, and translation of the works of the early and medieval church. Our efforts are to make the works of the church fathers accessible to anyone who might have an interest in Christian antiquities and the theological, philosophical, and moral writings that have become the bedrock of Western Civilization.

To-date, our releases have pulled from the Greek, Syriac, Georgian, Latin, Celtic, Ethiopian, and Coptic traditions of Christianity, and have been pulled from sundry local traditions and languages.

www.ingramcontent.com/pod-product-compliance
Lightning Source LLC
LaVergne TN
LVHW061041070526
838201LV00073B/5138